TAYLOR SWIFT QUIZ BOOK

101 Trivia Questions to Test Your Knowledge of Taylor Swift Facts

Lyrica Taytor

This Book Belongs To:

© Copyright 2023 - All rights reserved.

The content contained within this book may not be reproduced, duplicated or
transmitted without direct written permission from the author or the publisher.

Under no circumstances will any blame or legal responsibility be held against the publisher, or author, for any damages, reparation, or monetary loss due to the information contained within this book. Either directly or indirectly. You are responsible for your own choices, actions, and results.

Legal Notice:

This book is copyright protected. This book is only for personal use. You cannot amend, distribute, sell, use, quote or paraphrase any part, or the content within this book,
without the consent of the author or publisher.

Disclaimer Notice:

Please note the information contained within this document is for educational and entertainment purposes only. All effort has been executed to present accurate, up to date, and reliable, complete information. No warranties of any kind are declared or implied. Readers acknowledge that the author is not engaging in the rendering of legal, financial, medical or professional advice.

The content within this book has been derived
from various sources. Please consult a licensed professional before attempting any techniques outlined in this book.

By reading this document, the reader agrees that under no circumstances is the author responsible for any losses, direct or indirect, which are incurred as a result of the use of the information contained within this document, including, but not limited to, — errors, omissions, or inaccuracies.

1. *MULTIPLE CHOICE: EARLY BEGINNINGS*

Multiple Choice: What is Taylor Swift's middle name?
A) Elizabeth
B) Alison
C) Marie
D) Anne

2. *TRUE OR FALSE: EARLY BEGINNINGS*

True or False: Taylor Swift grew up on a Christmas tree farm.

Answers & Explanations!

QUESTION 1.
B)

Explanation: Taylor Swift's full name is Taylor Alison Swift. She was named after the singer-songwriter James Taylor.

QUESTION 2.
True!

Explanation: Taylor Swift spent her early years on a Christmas tree farm in Pennsylvania. This unique upbringing is often mentioned in her songs and interviews.

3. FILL IN THE BLANK:

Taylor Swift's 2020 album, "_____," won the Grammy Award for Album of the Year in 2021.

4. PICTURE THIS!

Which music video features Taylor Swift in a stunning ball gown, dancing in an ornate ballroom filled with mirrors?

Answers & Explanations!

QUESTION 3.
"Folklore"

Explanation: This album marked a significant stylistic shift for Taylor, featuring more indie folk and alternative rock elements.

QUESTION 4.
Love Story!

Explanation: This is a reference to the music video for "Love Story." The video is known for its fairy tale-like setting and romantic visuals, complementing the song's narrative.

5. MULTIPLE CHOICE: WHAT WAS IT??

Question: What was the title of Taylor Swift's debut single?
A) "Tim McGraw"
B) "Love Story"
C) "Teardrops on My Guitar"
D) "Our Song"

6. TRUE OR FALSE?: RECORD BREAKER

Question: Taylor Swift is the first female artist to win the Album of the Year Grammy Award three times.

Answers & Explanations!

QUESTION 5.
A)

Explanation: "Tim McGraw" was Taylor Swift's debut single, released in 2006. It marked the beginning of her journey to becoming a country and pop music icon.

QUESTION 6.
True!

Explanation: Taylor Swift made history by becoming the first woman to win the Album of the Year at the Grammys three times, achieving this with her albums "Fearless," "1989," and "Folklore."

7. MULTIPLE CHOICE: ACTING VENTURES

Question: Which movie did Taylor Swift make her acting debut in?
A) "Valentine's Day"
B) "The Giver"
C) "Cats"
D) "The Lorax"

8. TRUE OR FALSE: A YOUNG PRODIGY

Question: Taylor Swift wrote her first song, "Lucky You," when she was only 12 years old.

Answers & Explanations!

QUESTION 7.
A)
Explanation: Taylor Swift made her acting debut in the 2010 romantic comedy "Valentine's Day," showcasing her talent beyond music.

QUESTION 8.
True!
Explanation: Demonstrating her early songwriting talent, Taylor Swift wrote "Lucky You" at the age of 12, an early indicator of her exceptional skills in music and lyrics.

9. MULTIPLE CHOICE: INSPIRATION BEHIND THE HITS

Question: Which Taylor Swift song was inspired by a famous British actor she dated?
A) "Style"
B) "I Knew You Were Trouble"
C) "Back to December"
D) "Love Story"

10. MULTIPLE CHOICE: ICONIC ALBUMS

Question: Which album did Taylor Swift release in 2014, featuring the hit single "Shake It Off"?
A) "Red"
B) "1989"
C) "Reputation"
D) "Lover"

Answers & Explanations!

QUESTION 9.
A)
Explanation: "Style" is widely believed to be inspired by Harry Styles, a member of the boy band One Direction, whom Taylor Swift dated briefly.

QUESTION 10.
B)
Explanation: "1989," released in 2014, marked a significant shift in Taylor Swift's musical style from country to pop, with "Shake It Off" as one of its most popular tracks.

11. TRUE OR FALSE: SONGWRITING ACHIEVEMENT

Question: Taylor Swift wrote every song on her "Speak Now" album without any co-writers.

12. MULTIPLE CHOICE: COLLABORATION HITS

Question: Which song did Taylor Swift collaborate on with Ed Sheeran and Future?
A) "Everything Has Changed"
B) "End Game"
C) "Me!"
D) "I Don't Wanna Live Forever"

Answers & Explanations!

QUESTION 11.
True!

Explanation: Taylor Swift showcased her songwriting prowess by writing the entire "Speak Now" album on her own, a rare feat in the music industry.

QUESTION 12.
B)

Explanation: "End Game," a track from Taylor Swift's "Reputation" album, features collaborations with Ed Sheeran and Future, blending different musical styles.

13. TRUE OR FALSE: A UNIQUE RECORD LABEL

Question: Taylor Swift has always been signed to the same record label throughout her career.

14. MULTIPLE CHOICE: PHILANTHROPIC EFFORTS BREAKER

Question: Taylor Swift has been known for her charitable work. Which cause is she particularly known for supporting?
A) Animal rights
B) Education and literacy
C) Disaster relief
D) All of the above

Answers & Explanations!

QUESTION 13.
False!

Explanation: While Taylor Swift started her career with Big Machine Records, she later signed with Republic Records in 2018, marking a significant change in her career.

QUESTION 14.
D)

Explanation: Taylor Swift has been involved in various charitable efforts, including supporting animal rights, education and literacy programs, and disaster relief efforts, showcasing her commitment to giving back to the community.

15. MULTIPLE CHOICE: UNIQUE ACHIEVEMENTS

Taylor Swift is the only artist to have achieved what unique Billboard chart feat?
A) Debuted multiple albums at number one in the same year
B) Had all tracks from an album chart simultaneously
C) Won Billboard Woman of the Year three times
D) Had three albums each sell over a million copies in their first week

16. TRUE OR FALSE: A MUSICAL MILESTONE

Question: Taylor Swift's "Fearless" album is the most awarded country album in music history.

Answers & Explanations!

QUESTION 15.
C)
Explanation: Taylor Swift has been awarded Billboard Woman of the Year three times, an unprecedented achievement that highlights her influence in the music industry.

QUESTION 16.
True!
Explanation: "Fearless," released in 2008, has received widespread acclaim and numerous awards, making it the most awarded country album in music history.

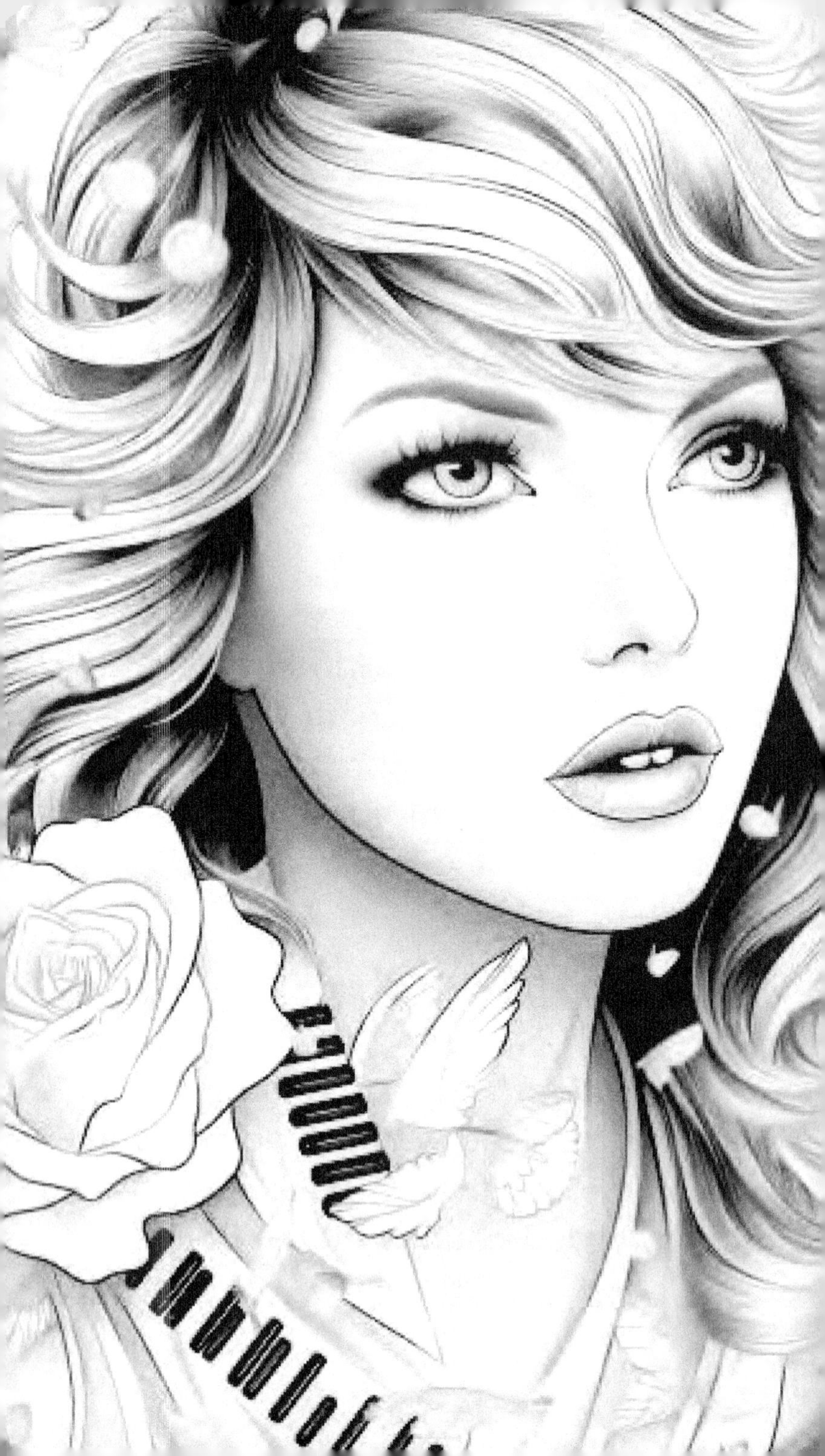

17. MULTIPLE CHOICE: FILM SOUNDTRACKS

Question: Which Taylor Swift song was featured in "The Hunger Games" movie soundtrack?
A) "Safe & Sound"
B) "Eyes Open"
C) "Today Was a Fairytale"
D) "Sweeter Than Fiction"

18. TRUE OR FALSE: A PROLIFIC WRITER

Question: Taylor Swift has written or co-written every song in her discography.

Answers & Explanations!

QUESTION 17.
A)
Explanation: "Safe & Sound," featuring The Civil Wars, was part of "The Hunger Games" soundtrack, showcasing Taylor Swift's versatility as an artist.

QUESTION 18.
True!
Explanation: Taylor Swift is known for her songwriting skills, having written or co-written every song she has released, a testament to her artistic authenticity.

19. MULTIPLE CHOICE: MUSICAL INFLUENCES

Question: Which legendary musician is known to be a major influence on Taylor Swift's songwriting?
A) Dolly Parton
B) Joni Mitchell
C) Carole King
D) Stevie Nicks

20. MULTIPLE CHOICE: GRAMMY RECORDS

Question: At what age did Taylor Swift become the youngest-ever winner of the Grammy Award for Album of the Year?
A) 18
B) 20
C) 22
D) 24

Answers & Explanations!

QUESTION 19.
B)
Explanation: Taylor Swift has cited Joni Mitchell as a significant influence on her songwriting style and artistic expression, particularly in her narrative lyricism.

QUESTION 20.
B)
Explanation: Taylor Swift won the Grammy for Album of the Year for "Fearless" at age 20, becoming the youngest artist at the time to win this prestigious award.

21. TRUE OR FALSE: MUSICAL GENRE SHIFT

Question: Taylor Swift's album "Folklore" marked her first foray into the indie folk genre.

22. TRUE OR FALSE: RECORD BREAKER

Multiple Choice: Early Life
Question: What was Taylor Swift's childhood dream job before becoming a singer-songwriter?
A) Actress
B) Novelist
C) Horseback rider
D) Veterinarian

Answers & Explanations!

QUESTION 21.
True!

Explanation: With "Folklore," released in 2020, Taylor Swift ventured into the indie folk genre, showcasing her versatility and ability to evolve her musical style.

QUESTION 22.
B)

Explanation: Before embarking on her music career, Taylor Swift aspired to be a novelist, reflecting her early love for storytelling and writing.

23. TRUE OR FALSE: A DISTINCTIVE HONOR

Question: Taylor Swift has a species of millipede named after her.

24. MULTIPLE CHOICE: PERSONAL LIFE

Question: Which city is Taylor Swift originally from?
A) Nashville, Tennessee
B) Reading, Pennsylvania
C) New York City, New York
D) Los Angeles, California

Answers & Explanations!

QUESTION 23.
True!

Explanation: Reflecting her wide-reaching impact, a species of millipede discovered in Tennessee was named Nannaria swiftae in honor of Taylor Swift.

QUESTION 24.
B)

Explanation: Taylor Swift was born and raised in Reading, Pennsylvania, before moving to Nashville, Tennessee, to pursue her music career.

25. MULTIPLE CHOICE: SIGNATURE INSTRUMENTS

Question: Which instrument is Taylor Swift famously known for playing during her performances?

A) Piano
B) Drums
C) Violin
D) Guitar

26. TRUE OR FALSE: A DEDICATED ARTIST

Question: Taylor Swift has re-recorded albums from her catalog to regain control over her masters.

Answers & Explanations!

QUESTION 25.
D)
Explanation: Taylor Swift is well-known for her skillful guitar playing, which has been a significant feature in many of her performances and music videos.

QUESTION 26.
True!
Explanation: In an effort to regain control over her music, Taylor Swift has embarked on re-recording her earlier albums, starting with "Fearless (Taylor's Version)."

27. MULTIPLE CHOICE: FAMOUS COLLABORATIONS

Question: With whom did Taylor Swift collaborate to create the hit song "I Don't Wanna Live Forever" for the film "Fifty Shades Darker"?

28. TRUE OR FALSE: A UNIQUE CHRISTMAS SONG

Question: Taylor Swift has a Christmas song titled "Christmas Tree Farm" that is based on her childhood experiences.

Answers & Explanations!

QUESTION 27.
B)
Explanation: Taylor Swift collaborated with Zayn Malik on the song "I Don't Wanna Live Forever," which was part of the soundtrack for the film "Fifty Shades Darker."

QUESTION 28.
True!
Explanation: "Christmas Tree Farm" is a Christmas song by Taylor Swift that draws inspiration from her childhood memories of growing up on a Christmas tree farm.

29. MULTIPLE CHOICE: INFLUENTIAL FIGURES

Question: Who did Taylor Swift name as her biggest musical influence?
A) Bruce Springsteen
B) Paul McCartney
C) Shania Twain
D) Madonna

30. MULTIPLE CHOICE: MUSIC VIDEO CAMEOS

Question: Which famous supermodel appeared in Taylor Swift's music video for "Bad Blood"?
A) Gigi Hadid
B) Cara Delevingne
C) Naomi Campbell
D) Kate Moss

Answers & Explanations!

QUESTION 29.
C)
Explanation: Taylor Swift has frequently named Shania Twain as her biggest musical influence, citing Twain's ability to blend country and pop music as a significant inspiration for her own career.

QUESTION 30.
B)
Explanation: Cara Delevingne is one of the many celebrities who made a cameo in Taylor Swift's star-studded music video for "Bad Blood."

31. TRUE OR FALSE: ACTING DEBUT

Question: Taylor Swift's acting debut was in the TV show "CSI: Crime Scene Investigation."

32. MULTIPLE CHOICE: ALBUM TITLES

Question: Which album did Taylor Swift release in 2014, featuring the hit single "Shake It Off"?
A) "Lover"
B) "Reputation"
C) "1989"
D) "Folklore"

Answers & Explanations!

QUESTION 31.
True!
Explanation: Taylor Swift made her acting debut in a 2009 episode of "CSI: Crime Scene Investigation," showcasing her talents beyond music.

QUESTION 32.
A)
Explanation: "Lover," released in 2019, is Taylor Swift's seventh studio album, featuring a colorful and romantic aesthetic distinct from her previous work.

33. TRUE OR FALSE: A LITERARY SONGWRITER

Question: Taylor Swift has a song inspired by a character from William Shakespeare's play. What is the songs name?

34. MULTIPLE CHOICE: PHILANTHROPIC CONTRIBUTIONS

Question: In response to the COVID-19 pandemic, Taylor Swift donated money to which cause?
A) Vaccine research
B) Providing personal protective equipment for healthcare workers
C) Supporting independent record stores
D) Aiding fans in financial hardship

Answers & Explanations!

QUESTION 33.
True!
Explanation: Taylor Swift's song "Love Story" is famously inspired by the characters Romeo and Juliet from William Shakespeare's play, but with a happy ending.

QUESTION 34.
D)
Explanation: During the COVID-19 pandemic, Taylor Swift notably provided financial support to fans experiencing hardship, demonstrating her compassion and connection with her fanbase.

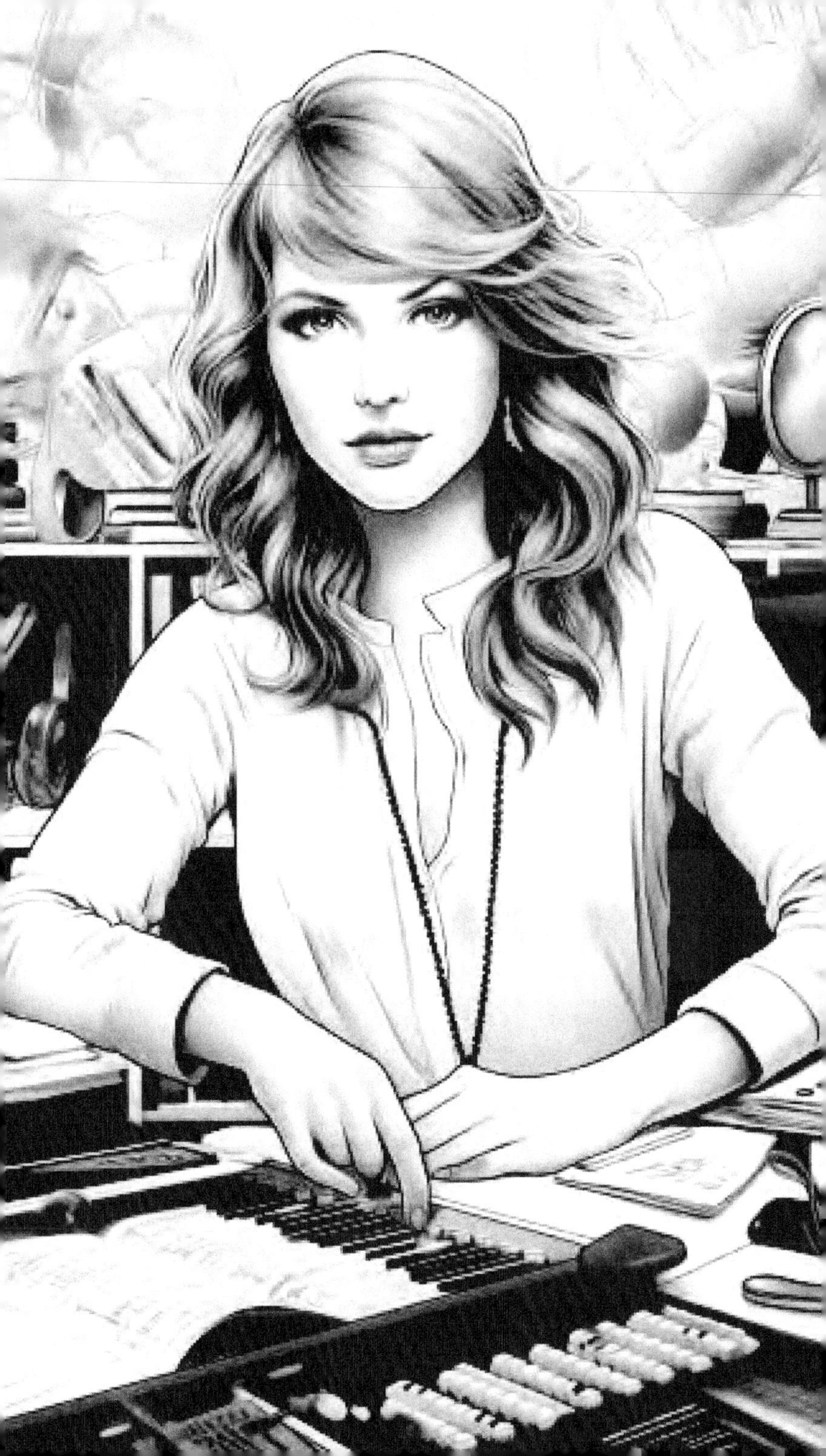

35. MULTIPLE CHOICE: CHART-TOPPING ACHIEVEMENTS

Question: Which Taylor Swift album made her the first female artist to have six albums each sell over a million copies in its first week?
A) "Reputation"
B) "1989"
C) "Lover"
D) "Folklore"

36. TRUE OR FALSE: A SYMBOL OF EMPOWERMENT

Question: Taylor Swift's song "The Man" explores themes of gender inequality and double standards in society.

Answers & Explanations!

QUESTION 35.
A)
Explanation: Taylor Swift's album "Reputation" achieved the milestone of making her the first female artist to have six consecutive albums sell over a million copies in their first week.

QUESTION 36.
True!
Explanation: "The Man" is a song by Taylor Swift that addresses gender inequality and societal double standards, showcasing her use of music as a platform for social commentary.

37. MULTIPLE CHOICE: EARLY ACHIEVEMENTS

Question: At what age did Taylor Swift sign her first record deal?

A) 14
B) 15
C) 16
D) 17

38. TRUE OR FALSE: A UNIQUE SONGWRITING STYLE

Question: Taylor Swift has a tradition of including secret messages in the lyrics of her album booklets.

Answers & Explanations!

QUESTION 37.
B)
Explanation: Taylor Swift signed her first record deal at age 15 with Big Machine Records, starting her journey to becoming a music sensation.

QUESTION 38.
True!
Explanation: Known for her unique songwriting style, Taylor Swift has included secret messages within the lyrics printed in her album booklets, adding an extra layer of meaning for her fans.

39. *MULTIPLE CHOICE: INFLUENCES AND MENTORS*

Question: Which famous country singer is known to have been an early mentor to Taylor Swift?
A) Faith Hill
B) Carrie Underwood
C) Garth Brooks
D) Brad Paisley

40. *MULTIPLE CHOICE: GLOBAL TOURS*

Question: What was the name of Taylor Swift's first world tour?
A) The Fearless Tour
B) The Red Tour
C) The Speak Now World Tour
D) The 1989 World Tour

Answers & Explanations!

QUESTION 39.
A)
Explanation: Faith Hill, among other artists, is known to have been an early mentor to Taylor Swift, helping guide her in the early stages of her career in country music.

QUESTION 40.
A)
Explanation: The Fearless Tour was Taylor Swift's first headlining world tour, supporting her album "Fearless." It showcased her rise as a global star in the music industry.

41. TRUE OR FALSE: A PIONEERING MUSICIAN

Question: Taylor Swift is the first and only female artist in the 21st century to have an album on the Billboard 200 for 400 weeks.

42. MULTIPLE CHOICE: SONGWRITING HONORS

Question: Which prestigious songwriting hall of fame inducted Taylor Swift as the youngest ever entrant?
A) The Songwriters Hall of Fame
B) The Nashville Songwriters Hall of Fame
C) The Country Music Hall of Fame
D) The Rock & Roll Hall of Fame

Answers & Explanations!

QUESTION 41.
True!
Explanation: Taylor Swift achieved this remarkable feat with her album "Fearless," highlighting her lasting impact and popularity in the music world.

QUESTION 42.
B)
Explanation: Taylor Swift was inducted into the Nashville Songwriters Hall of Fame as the youngest ever entrant, a testament to her extraordinary songwriting talent.

43. TRUE OR FALSE: AN ECLECTIC MUSIC VIDEO DIRECTOR

Question: Taylor Swift has directed some of her own music videos.

44. MULTIPLE CHOICE: ADVOCACY AND VOICE

Question: Taylor Swift has been vocal about which political issue?
A) Climate change
B) LGBTQ+ rights
C) Education reform
D) All of the above

Answers & Explanations!

QUESTION 43.
True!

Explanation: In addition to her musical talents, Taylor Swift has also directed several of her music videos, showcasing her creative vision and artistic control.

QUESTION 44.
D)

Explanation: Taylor Swift has used her platform to advocate for various political issues, including climate change, LGBTQ+ rights, and education reform, demonstrating her commitment to social and political activism.

45. MULTIPLE CHOICE: FAMOUS COLLABORATIONS

Question: Taylor Swift collaborated with which legendary folk artist on her album "Evermore"?

A) Bob Dylan
B) Joni Mitchell
C) Bon Iver
D) James Taylor

46. TRUE OR FALSE: A UNIQUE RECORD LABEL MOVE

Question: Taylor Swift created her own record label to release her future albums.

Answers & Explanations!

QUESTION 45.
C)
Explanation: Taylor Swift collaborated with Bon Iver on the song "Exile," featured on her "Evermore" album, which was praised for its haunting and emotive duet.

QUESTION 46.
False!
Explanation: While Taylor Swift has been very proactive about her music rights, she did not create her own label; instead, she signed with Republic Records after leaving Big Machine Records.

47. MULTIPLE CHOICE: MUSIC VIDEO DIRECTING

Question: Which music video, directed by Taylor Swift, won the Best Direction award at the MTV Video Music Awards?
A) "You Need to Calm Down"
B) "The Man"
C) "Cardigan"
D) "Willow"

48. TRUE OR FALSE: A TRIBUTE TO A LITERARY CLASSIC

Question: Taylor Swift's song "Love Story" includes a reference to the classic novel "Pride and Prejudice" by Jane Austen.

Answers & Explanations!

QUESTION 47.
C)
Explanation: The music video for "Cardigan," directed by Taylor Swift, won the Best Direction award at the MTV Video Music Awards, highlighting her skills as a music video director.

QUESTION 48.
True!
Explanation: In "Love Story," Taylor Swift references "Pride and Prejudice," drawing a parallel between her song's narrative and the classic love story in Jane Austen's novel.

49. *MULTIPLE CHOICE: EARLY CAREER INFLUENCES*

Question: Which artist did Taylor Swift open for during her early days as a country music artist?
A) Tim McGraw
B) Rascal Flatts
C) George Strait
D) Kenny Chesney

50. *MULTIPLE CHOICE: CHILDHOOD AMBITIONS*

Question: What hobby did Taylor Swift particularly enjoy during her childhood, which is often reflected in her songwriting?
A) Painting
B) Horseback riding
C) Creative writing
D) Acting

Answers & Explanations!

QUESTION 49.
B)
Explanation: Early in her career, Taylor Swift opened for Rascal Flatts on their tour, providing her with significant exposure and experience in the country music scene.

QUESTION 50.
C)
Explanation: Taylor Swift was passionate about creative writing during her childhood, often writing poems and stories, a hobby that undoubtedly contributed to her exceptional songwriting skills.

51. TRUE OR FALSE: MUSICAL RANGE

Question: Taylor Swift has experimented with genres outside of country and pop, including rock and electronic music.

52. MULTIPLE CHOICE: SIGNATURE SONGS BREAKER

Question: Which song did Taylor Swift perform during the 2010 Grammy Awards that marked a significant moment in her early career?
A) "Fearless"
B) "You Belong With Me"
C) "Fifteen"
D) "White Horse"

Answers & Explanations!

QUESTION 51.
True
Explanation: Taylor Swift has explored various music genres throughout her career, including forays into rock and electronic music, showcasing her versatility as an artist.

QUESTION 52.
C)
Explanation: Taylor Swift's performance of "Fifteen" at the 2010 Grammy Awards was a notable early career moment, highlighting her rising status in the music industry.

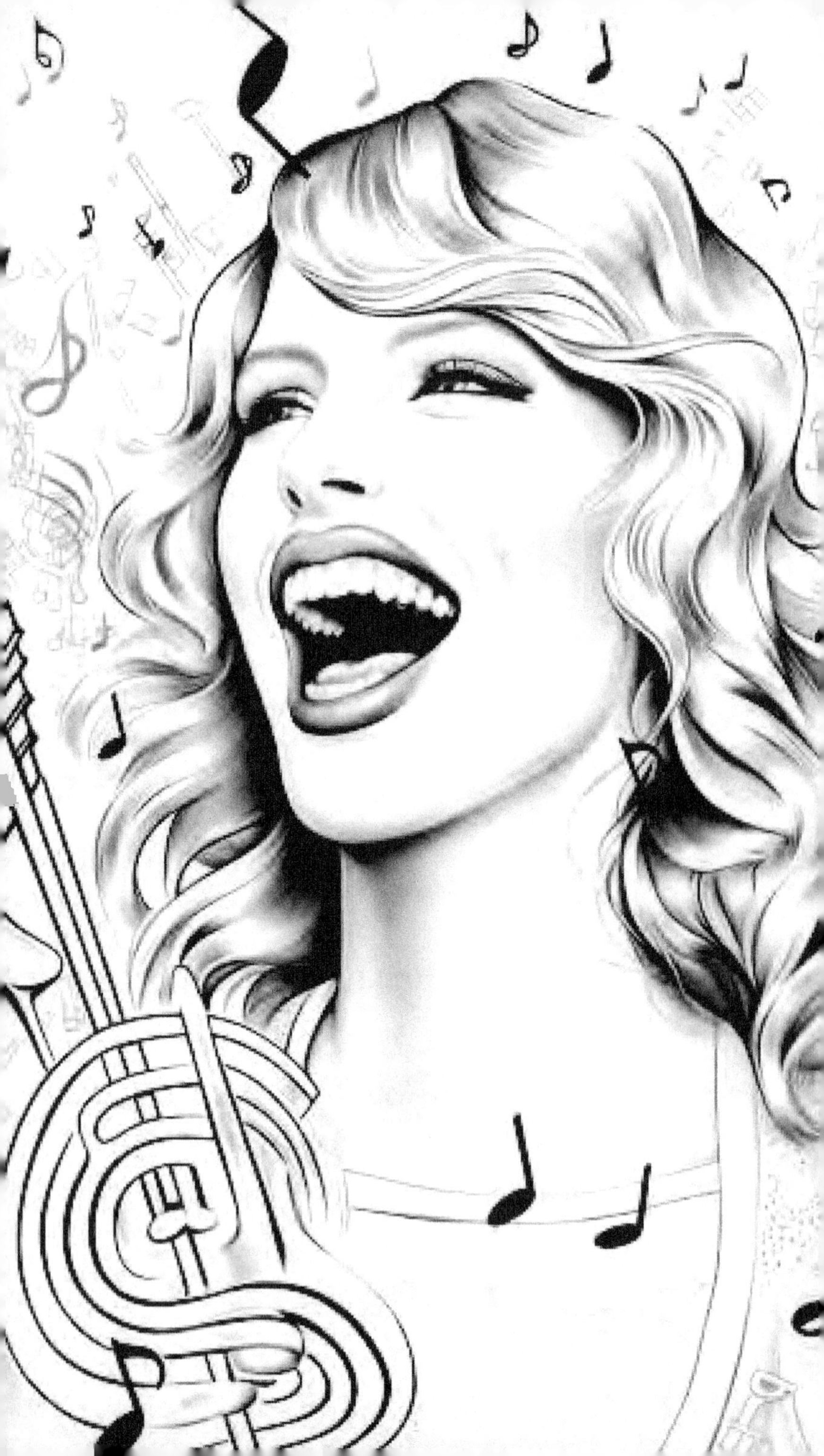

53. TRUE OR FALSE: RECOGNITION IN SONGWRITING

Question: Taylor Swift has been awarded the Songwriter/Artist of the Year by the Nashville Songwriters Association International more than any other artist.

54. MULTIPLE CHOICE: INSPIRATIONAL FIGURES

Question: Taylor Swift once said, "No matter what happens in life, be good to people. Being good to people is a wonderful legacy to leave behind." In which context did she say this?
A) In a magazine interview
B) During a concert
C) In her documentary "Miss Americana"
D) Accepting an award

Answers & Explanations!

QUESTION 53.
True!

Explanation: Taylor Swift has received the Songwriter/Artist of the Year award from the Nashville Songwriters Association International multiple times, more than any other artist, underlining her significant contributions to songwriting.

QUESTION 54.
A)

Explanation: Taylor Swift shared this inspirational quote during a magazine interview, reflecting her personal philosophy and approach to life, emphasizing kindness and the importance of how we treat others.

55. MULTIPLE CHOICE: INSPIRATIONAL FIGURES

Question: Which classic American writer has Taylor Swift cited as a major influence on her storytelling style?

A) Mark Twain
B) F. Scott Fitzgerald
C) Ernest Hemingway
D) Harper Lee

56. MULTIPLE CHOICE: BELOVED PETS

Question: What is the name of one of Taylor Swift's famous pet cats?

A) Daisy
B) Olivia Benson
C) Mr. Whiskers
D) Luna

Answers & Explanations!

QUESTION 55.
A)
Explanation: Taylor Swift has expressed admiration for Mark Twain's storytelling abilities, citing his work as an influence on her narrative songwriting style.

QUESTION 56.
B)
Explanation: Taylor Swift has a beloved cat named Olivia Benson, named after the character from the TV show "Law & Order: SVU." Olivia has even appeared in some of Swift's social media posts and music videos.

57. TRUE OR FALSE: CULINARY SKILLS

Question: Taylor Swift enjoys baking and often shares her homemade treats with friends and family.

58. MULTIPLE CHOICE: CHILDHOOD ACTIVITIES

Question: As a child, Taylor Swift grew up on a farm where she helped with what kind of Trees?
A) Blue Gum
B) Loblolly Pine
C) Red Maple
D) Christmas Trees

Answers & Explanations!

QUESTION 57.
True

Explanation: Taylor Swift is known for her love of baking, often whipping up cookies, cakes, and other treats for her loved ones.

QUESTION 58.
D)

Explanation: Taylor Swift grew up on a Christmas tree farm in Pennsylvania, where she helped with the family Christmas tree business during her childhood.

59. TRUE OR FALSE: A KEEN READER

Question: Taylor Swift is an avid reader and often draws inspiration from literature for her songs.

60. MULTIPLE CHOICE: ROAD TRIP TUNES

Question: What genre of music does Taylor Swift prefer to listen to while driving?
A) Country
B) Hip-hop
C) Classic rock
D) Pop

Answers & Explanations!

QUESTION 59.
True
Explanation: Taylor Swift is an avid reader and often draws inspiration from literature for her songs.

QUESTION 60.
B)
Explanation: Explanation: Taylor Swift has mentioned in interviews that she enjoys listening to hip-hop music while driving, citing it as a favorite for car trips.

61. TRUE OR FALSE: A PHILANTHROPIC HEART

Question: Taylor Swift has a history of making anonymous donations to causes and individuals in need.

62. MULTIPLE CHOICE: FAVORITE HOLIDAY

Question: What is Taylor Swift's favorite holiday, which she often celebrates with themed parties and decorations?
A) Christmas
B) Halloween
C) Fourth of July
D) Thanksgiving

Answers & Explanations!

QUESTION 61.
True!
Explanation: Taylor Swift is known for her philanthropy, often making generous and sometimes anonymous donations to various causes and individuals, reflecting her commitment to helping others.

QUESTION 62.
C)
Explanation: Taylor Swift is famous for her Fourth of July parties, often celebrated with friends and elaborate decorations, showcasing her love for this holiday.

63. TRUE OR FALSE: A PASSION FOR PAINTING

Question: In addition to music, Taylor Swift is also passionate about painting and visual arts.

64. MULTIPLE CHOICE: EARLY CAREER DECISION

Question: Before focusing on a career in music, what profession did Taylor Swift consider pursuing?
A) Journalism
B) Acting
C) Law
D) Teaching

Answers & Explanations!

QUESTION 63.
True!

Explanation: Taylor Swift has shown a keen interest in painting and visual arts, often engaging in these activities as a hobby outside of her music career.

QUESTION 64.
A)

Explanation: Taylor Swift had considered a career in journalism before deciding to pursue music, reflecting her interest in storytelling and writing.

65. TRUE OR FALSE: A LOVE FOR HORSES

Question: Taylor Swift has a long-standing love for horses and used to ride competitively as a teenager.

66. MULTIPLE CHOICE: CHILDHOOD DREAMS

Question: What was Taylor Swift's favorite subject in school?
A) English
B) Mathematics
C) History
D) Science

Answers & Explanations!

QUESTION 65.
True!
Explanation: Before her music career took off, Taylor Swift was an avid horseback rider and competed in equestrian events, showcasing her diverse range of interests from a young age.

QUESTION 66.
A)
Explanation: Taylor Swift has expressed that English was her favorite subject in school, aligning with her passion for storytelling and songwriting.

67. TRUE OR FALSE: A DEDICATED FRIEND

Question: Taylor Swift is known for maintaining close friendships with several high-profile celebrities.

68. MULTIPLE CHOICE: INFLUENTIAL ENCOUNTERS

Question: Who was the music manager that discovered Taylor Swift at a cafe performance?
A) Scott Borchetta
B) Simon Fuller
C) Joe Galante
D) Scooter Braun

Answers & Explanations!

QUESTION 67.
True!
Explanation: Taylor Swift is famous for her close-knit circle of friends, which includes various celebrities, showcasing her value for deep and lasting friendships.

QUESTION 68.
A)
Explanation: Taylor Swift was discovered by music manager Scott Borchetta during a performance at The Bluebird Café in Nashville, which led to her first record deal.

69. TRUE OR FALSE: FAMILY TIES

Question: Taylor Swift has a brother who is also involved in the entertainment industry.

70. MULTIPLE CHOICE: A SPECIAL NUMBER

Question: What is Taylor Swift's favorite number, often referenced in her work?
A) 7
B) 13
C) 22
D) 1989

Answers & Explanations!

QUESTION 69.
True!

Explanation: Taylor Swift's brother, Austin Swift, is involved in the entertainment industry, pursuing a career in acting.

QUESTION 70.
B)

Explanation: Taylor Swift's favorite number is 13. She considers it her lucky number and often references it in her music and personal life.

71. TRUE OR FALSE: A MULTILINGUAL TALENT

Question: Taylor Swift is fluent in more than one language.

72. MULTIPLE CHOICE: PERSONAL FASHION STYLE

Question: How would Taylor Swift describe her own fashion style?
A) Classic and vintage
B) Edgy and modern
C) Casual and comfortable
D) Bold and eclectic

Answers & Explanations!

QUESTION 71.
False!
Explanation: While Taylor Swift has shown interest in learning other languages, she is not fluently multilingual.

QUESTION 72.
D)
Explanation: Taylor Swift has described her fashion style as bold and eclectic, reflecting her willingness to experiment with different looks and styles.

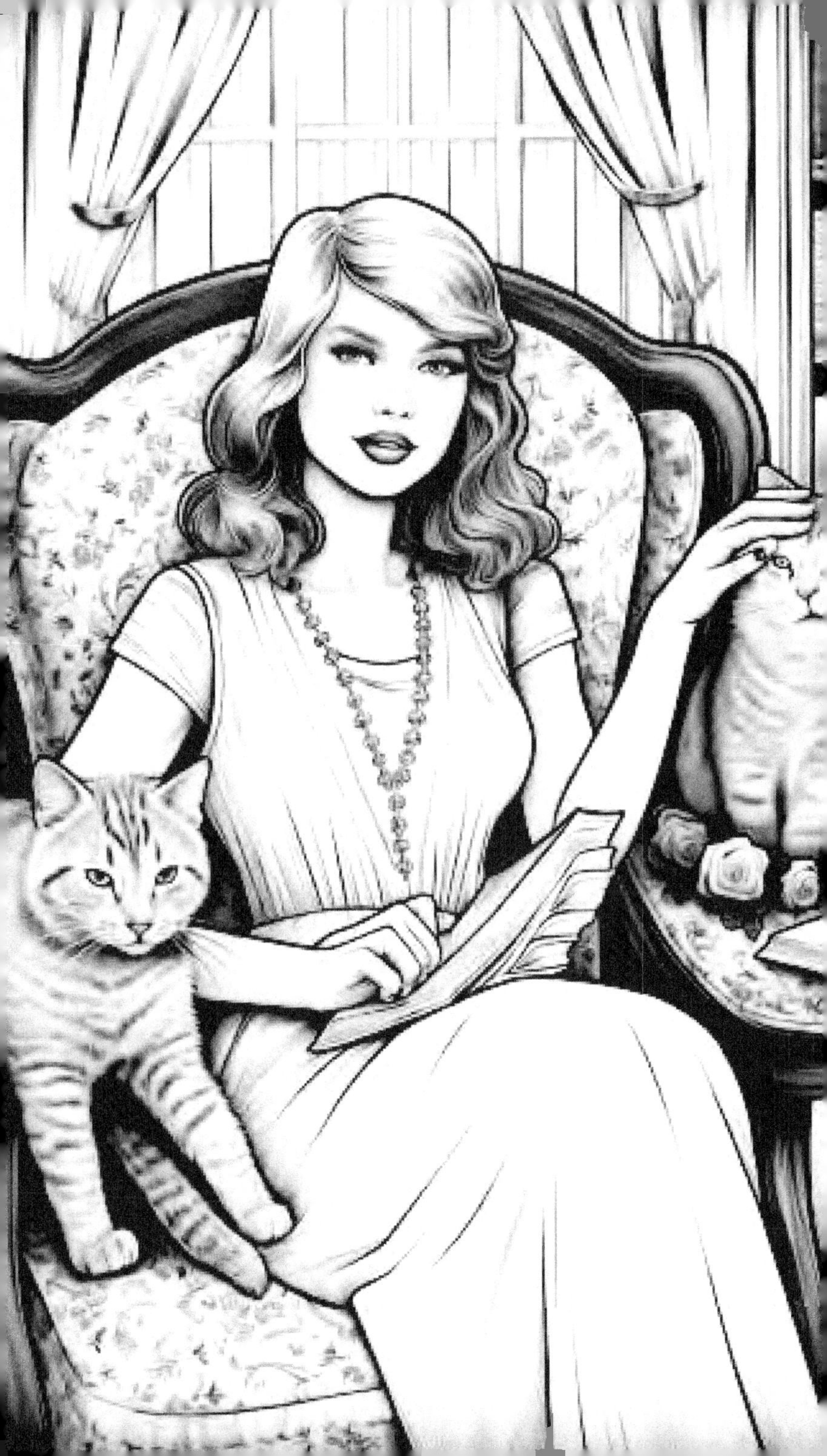

73. TRUE OR FALSE: AN ENVIRONMENTAL ADVOCATE

Question: Taylor Swift actively supports environmental causes and sustainability.

74. MULTIPLE CHOICE: AVID COLLECTION

Question: What unusual item is Taylor Swift known to collect?
A) Vintage guitars
B) Snow globes
C) Antique mirrors
D) Classic vinyl records

Answers & Explanations!

QUESTION 73.
True!
Explanation: Before her music career took off, Taylor Swift was an avid horseback rider and competed in equestrian events, showcasing her diverse range of interests from a young age.

QUESTION 74.
B)
Explanation: Taylor Swift has a unique hobby of collecting snow globes, a collection she's talked about in interviews.

75. TRUE OR FALSE: A SUPPORTER OF EDUCATION

Question: Taylor Swift has donated funds to support education, including contributions to schools and libraries.

76. MULTIPLE CHOICE: EARLY INSPIRATIONS

A) Dolly Parton
B) Faith Hill
C) Shania Twain
D) Reba McEntire

Answers & Explanations!

QUESTION 75.
True!

Explanation: Taylor Swift has made several donations to support education, including contributions to schools and public libraries, highlighting her commitment to literacy and learning.

QUESTION 76.
C)

Explanation: Taylor Swift has often cited Shania Twain as a major influence on her decision to pursue country music. Twain's successful crossover into pop music inspired Swift to blend genres in her own career.

77. TRUE OR FALSE: MUSICAL VARIETY

Question: Taylor Swift has only ever released albums in the country and pop genres.

78. MULTIPLE CHOICE: AWARD MILESTONES

Question: Which album earned Taylor Swift her first Grammy Award for Album of the Year?
A) "Taylor Swift"
B) "Fearless"
C) "Speak Now"
D) "Red"

Answers & Explanations!

QUESTION 77.

False!

Explanation: Taylor Swift has explored various genres throughout her career, not just limiting herself to country and pop. Albums like "Folklore" and "Evermore" venture into indie folk, alternative rock, and electro-folk, showcasing her versatility as an artist.

QUESTION 78.

B)

Explanation: Taylor Swift's album "Fearless" won the Grammy Award for Album of the Year in 2010, making her the youngest artist at the time to win this prestigious award. The album, which includes hits like "Love Story" and "You Belong With Me," solidified her status as a crossover sensation.

79. MULTIPLE CHOICE: RARE PERFORMANCES

Question: Which song, a rare live performance by Taylor Swift, is about a young boy who passed away from neuroblastoma?

A) "Ronan"
B) "Soon You'll Get Better"
C) "The Best Day"
D) "Never Grow Up"

80. MULTIPLE CHOICE: SIGNATURE SONGWRITING

Question: Taylor Swift is known for incorporating what distinctive feature in her songwriting?

A) Complex metaphors
B) Personal experiences and relationships
C) Historical references
D) Science fiction themes

Answers & Explanations!

QUESTION 79.
A)
Explanation: "Ronan" is a song Taylor Swift performed live only a few times, dedicated to a four-year-old boy named Ronan who died from neuroblastoma. The song's heartfelt and emotional lyrics reflect Swift's ability to convey deep empathy and compassion through her music.

QUESTION 80.
B)
Explanation: Taylor Swift is renowned for her songwriting style that often includes narratives about her personal experiences and relationships. This approach has created a deep connection with her audience, as her songs reflect genuine emotions and experiences many can relate to.

81. MULTIPLE CHOICE: CINEMATIC CONTRIBUTIONS

Question: For which film did Taylor Swift co-write and perform the song "Safe & Sound"?
A) "The Fault in Our Stars"
B) "The Hunger Games"
C) "Twilight"
D) "Divergent"

82. TRUE OR FALSE: A SYMBOL OF ARTISTIC CONTROL

Question: Taylor Swift's album "Lover" was the first album she owned the masters to.

Answers & Explanations!

QUESTION 81.

B)

Explanation: Taylor Swift co-wrote and performed "Safe & Sound" for "The Hunger Games" movie soundtrack. The song, featuring The Civil Wars, perfectly captured the film's solemn and haunting atmosphere, adding depth to its narrative.

QUESTION 82.

True!

Explanation: "Lover," released in 2019, was the first album for which Taylor Swift owned the master recordings outright. This was a significant milestone in her career, representing her ongoing efforts to maintain artistic and financial control over her work.

83. MULTIPLE CHOICE: UNIQUE SONG CHARACTERISTICS

Question: In which song does Taylor Swift use the sound of a heartbeat as an instrument?
A) "Wildest Dreams"
B) "I Knew You Were Trouble"
C) "Style"
D) "Delicate"

84. TRUE OR FALSE: A PASSION FOR ACTING

Question: Alongside her music career, Taylor Swift has pursued acting, appearing in various films and television shows.

Answers & Explanations!

QUESTION 83.

A)

Explanation: In "Wildest Dreams," Taylor Swift creatively uses the sound of a heartbeat as part of the song's instrumentation. This artistic choice adds a unique and personal touch to the track, showcasing her innovative approach to music production.

QUESTION 84.

True!

Explanation: Taylor Swift has explored acting alongside her music career, appearing in films like "Valentine's Day" and "The Giver," as well as guest appearances on television shows, demonstrating her versatility as an entertainer.

85. MULTIPLE CHOICE: UNIQUE ACHIEVEMENTS

Question: Taylor Swift set a record for the most American Music Awards won by a female artist in a single night. How many awards did she win?

A) 4
B) 6
C) 8
D) 10

86. MULTIPLE CHOICE: EARLY PERFORMANCES

Question: Taylor Swift first gained public attention when she performed the national anthem at what sports event?

A) A Philadelphia 76ers basketball game
B) A Pittsburgh Steelers football game
C) A Philadelphia Flyers hockey match
D) The Tennis U.S. Open

Answers & Explanations!

QUESTION 66.
B)
Explanation: Taylor Swift set a record at the American Music Awards by winning 6 awards in one night. This achievement highlighted her popularity and critical acclaim, as well as her significant impact on the music industry.

QUESTION 86.
A)
Explanation: One of Taylor Swift's early public performances was singing the national anthem at a Philadelphia 76ers NBA game. This event was significant in showcasing her talent to a broader audience at a young age.

87. TRUE OR FALSE: ARTISTIC ACKNOWLEDGMENT

Question: Taylor Swift has been named Time magazine's Person of the Year.

88. MULTIPLE CHOICE: FILM SOUNDTRACK APPEARANCES

Question: Taylor Swift contributed to the soundtrack of which animated movie with the song "Sweeter than Fiction"?
A) "Frozen"
B) "Tangled"
C) "One Chance"
D) "Brave"

Answers & Explanations!

QUESTION 87.
True!

Explanation: Taylor Swift was recognized as one of Time magazine's "Persons of the Year" in 2017 as part of the "Silence Breakers," acknowledging her contributions to the #MeToo movement and her stance against sexual harassment.

QUESTION 88.
C)

Explanation: "Sweeter than Fiction" is a song by Taylor Swift for the soundtrack of the film "One Chance." The song showcases her ability to create music that complements cinematic stories.

89. TRUE OR FALSE: A CULTURAL ICON

Question: Taylor Swift has been inducted into the Songwriters Hall of Fame.

90. MULTIPLE CHOICE: HONORARY TITLES

Question: Which university awarded Taylor Swift an honorary Doctorate of Fine Arts degree?
A) Harvard University
B) University of Pennsylvania
C) New York University
D) Vanderbilt University

Answers & Explanations!

QUESTION 89.
False!
Explanation: While Taylor Swift has received numerous awards and accolades for her songwriting, as of my last update, she has not yet been inducted into the Songwriters Hall of Fame.

QUESTION 90.
C)
Explanation: New York University awarded Taylor Swift an honorary Doctorate of Fine Arts degree in recognition of her significant contributions to music and culture. This honor underscores her influence and achievements in the arts.

91. MULTIPLE CHOICE: SONGWRITING PARTNERSHIPS

Question: With which artist did Taylor Swift co-write the song "This Is What You Came For" under a pseudonym?
A) Calvin Harris
B) Ed Sheeran
C) Kendrick Lamar
D) John Mayer

92. TRUE OR FALSE: HISTORICAL RECOGNITION

Question: Taylor Swift is the first female solo artist to win two MTV Video Music Awards for Video of the Year.

Answers & Explanations!

QUESTION 91.
A)
Explanation: Taylor Swift co-wrote the song "This Is What You Came For" with Calvin Harris under the pseudonym Nils Sjöberg. This collaboration was initially kept secret, showcasing her ability to diversify her songwriting contributions.

QUESTION 92.
True!
Explanation: Taylor Swift achieved the distinction of being the first female solo artist to win two MTV Video Music Awards for Video of the Year, for her videos "Bad Blood" and "You Need to Calm Down," highlighting her significant impact in the realm of music videos.

93. MULTIPLE CHOICE: CHARITY CONCERTS

Question: Taylor Swift performed a charity concert to benefit victims of what natural disaster?

A) 2010 Haiti earthquake
B) 2011 Japan earthquake and tsunami
C) 2013 Typhoon Haiyan in the Philippines
D) 2017 Hurricane Harvey

94. TRUE OR FALSE: ACTING RANGE

Question: Taylor Swift has voiced a character in an animated movie.

Answers & Explanations!

QUESTION 93.
B)

Explanation: In response to the 2011 Japan earthquake and tsunami, Taylor Swift performed a charity concert and donated all proceeds to the relief efforts. This event is a testament to her commitment to humanitarian causes.

QUESTION 94.
True!

Explanation: Taylor Swift lent her voice to a character in the animated movie "The Lorax," further showcasing her versatility in the entertainment industry beyond her music career.

95. TRUE OR FALSE: SONGWRITING MILESTONES

Question: Taylor Swift wrote the song "Better Than Revenge" in under 30 minutes.

96. MULTIPLE CHOICE: UNIQUE SONG FEATURES

Question: In which Taylor Swift song does a voicemail message feature prominently?
A) "We Are Never Ever Getting Back Together"
B) "All Too Well"
C) "I Almost Do"
D) "I Forgot That You Existed"

Answers & Explanations!

QUESTION 95.
True!

Explanation: Taylor Swift is known for her rapid songwriting ability, and she wrote "Better Than Revenge" in under 30 minutes. This feat demonstrates her natural talent for crafting lyrics and melodies quickly.

QUESTION 96.
B)

Explanation: In "All Too Well," a voicemail message is incorporated into the song, adding an element of personal and emotional depth. This feature makes the song uniquely poignant and memorable.

97. MULTIPLE CHOICE: COLLABORATION HITS

Question: Which song did Taylor Swift collaborate on with Ed Sheeran and Future?

98. MULTIPLE CHOICE: THEATRICAL PERFORMANCES

Question: Which classic play did Taylor Swift perform in during her high school years?
A) "Romeo and Juliet"
B) "The Sound of Music"
C) "Bye Bye Birdie"
D) "Grease"

Answers & Explanations!

QUESTION 97.
B)
Explanation: "End Game," a track from Taylor Swift's "Reputation" album, features collaborations with Ed Sheeran and Future, blending different musical styles.

QUESTION 98.
C)
Explanation: During her high school years, Taylor Swift performed in a production of the classic play "Bye Bye Birdie." Her involvement in theatrical performances during her youth showcases her early interest in performing arts beyond music.

99. MULTIPLE CHOICE: TOURING MILESTONES

Question: In 2009, Taylor Swift served as a supporting act for which artist's world tour?
A) Brad Paisley
B) Keith Urban
C) Carrie Underwood
D) Kenny Chesney

100. MULTIPLE CHOICE: FAN BASE ORIGINS

Question: The term "Swifties" is widely used to describe Taylor Swift's fans. How did this term come into popular usage?
A) It was coined by Taylor Swift in an interview.
B) Fans themselves started using it on social media.
C) It originated from a contest held by Taylor Swift.
D) It was first used in a magazine article about Taylor Swift.

Answers & Explanations!

QUESTION 99.
B)

Explanation: In 2009, Taylor Swift joined Keith Urban's Escape Together World Tour as a supporting act. This experience was significant in her early career, providing her the opportunity to perform in front of large audiences and gain wider exposure, further establishing her as a rising star in the country music scene.

QUESTION 100.
B)

Explanation: The term "Swifties" to describe Taylor Swift's fans originated organically among the fans themselves, primarily through social media platforms. As the fan community grew and connected online, they adopted this nickname as a way to identify themselves and their shared admiration for Taylor Swift. This term reflects the close-knit and passionate nature of her fan base.

101. WHAT IS YOUR TRIVIA QUESTION? WRITE IT DOWN BELOW AND ASK YOUR FRIENDS!

Question:

_____
_____
_____
_____

OPTION A:_____   OPTION B:_____
_____   _____

OPTION C:_____   OPTION D:_____
_____   _____

ANSWER:

_____
_____
_____
_____
_____
_____

102. WHAT IS YOUR TRIVIA QUESTION? WRITE IT DOWN BELOW AND ASK YOUR FRIENDS!

Question:
_____
_____
_____
_____

OPTION A: _____
_____

OPTION B: _____
_____

OPTION C: _____
_____

OPTION D: _____
_____

ANSWER:
_____
_____
_____
_____
_____

103. WHAT IS YOUR TRIVIA QUESTION? WRITE IT DOWN BELOW AND ASK YOUR FRIENDS!

Question:

_____

OPTION A: _____

OPTION B: _____

OPTION C: _____

OPTION D: _____

ANSWER:

_____

104. WHAT IS YOUR TRIVIA QUESTION? WRITE IT DOWN BELOW AND ASK YOUR FRIENDS!

Question:

_____
_____
_____
_____

OPTION A: _____

OPTION B: _____

OPTION C: _____

OPTION D: _____

ANSWER:

_____
_____
_____
_____
_____

105. *WHAT IS YOUR TRIVIA QUESTION? WRITE IT DOWN BELOW AND ASK YOUR FRIENDS!*

Question:

_____

_____

_____

_____

OPTION A: _____

OPTION B: _____

OPTION C: _____

OPTION D: _____

ANSWER:

_____

_____

_____

_____

106. WHAT IS YOUR TRIVIA QUESTION? WRITE IT DOWN BELOW AND ASK YOUR FRIENDS!

Question:
_____

OPTION A: _____

OPTION B: _____

OPTION C: _____

OPTION D: _____

ANSWER:
_____

107. WHAT IS YOUR TRIVIA QUESTION? WRITE IT DOWN BELOW AND ASK YOUR FRIENDS!

Question:
_____
_____
_____
_____

OPTION A: _____

OPTION B: _____

OPTION C: _____

OPTION D: _____

ANSWER:
_____
_____
_____
_____
_____
_____

108. WHAT IS YOUR TRIVIA QUESTION? WRITE IT DOWN BELOW AND ASK YOUR FRIENDS!

Question:
_____
_____
_____
_____

OPTION A: _____
OPTION B: _____

OPTION C: _____
OPTION D: _____

ANSWER:
_____
_____
_____
_____
_____

109. WHAT IS YOUR TRIVIA QUESTION? WRITE IT DOWN BELOW AND ASK YOUR FRIENDS!

Question:

_____

_____

_____

_____

OPTION A: _____

OPTION B: _____

OPTION C: _____

OPTION D: _____

ANSWER:

_____

_____

_____

_____

_____

110. *WHAT IS YOUR TRIVIA QUESTION? WRITE IT DOWN BELOW AND ASK YOUR FRIENDS!*

Question:

___

OPTION A:___

OPTION B:___

OPTION C:___

OPTION D:___

ANSWER:

___

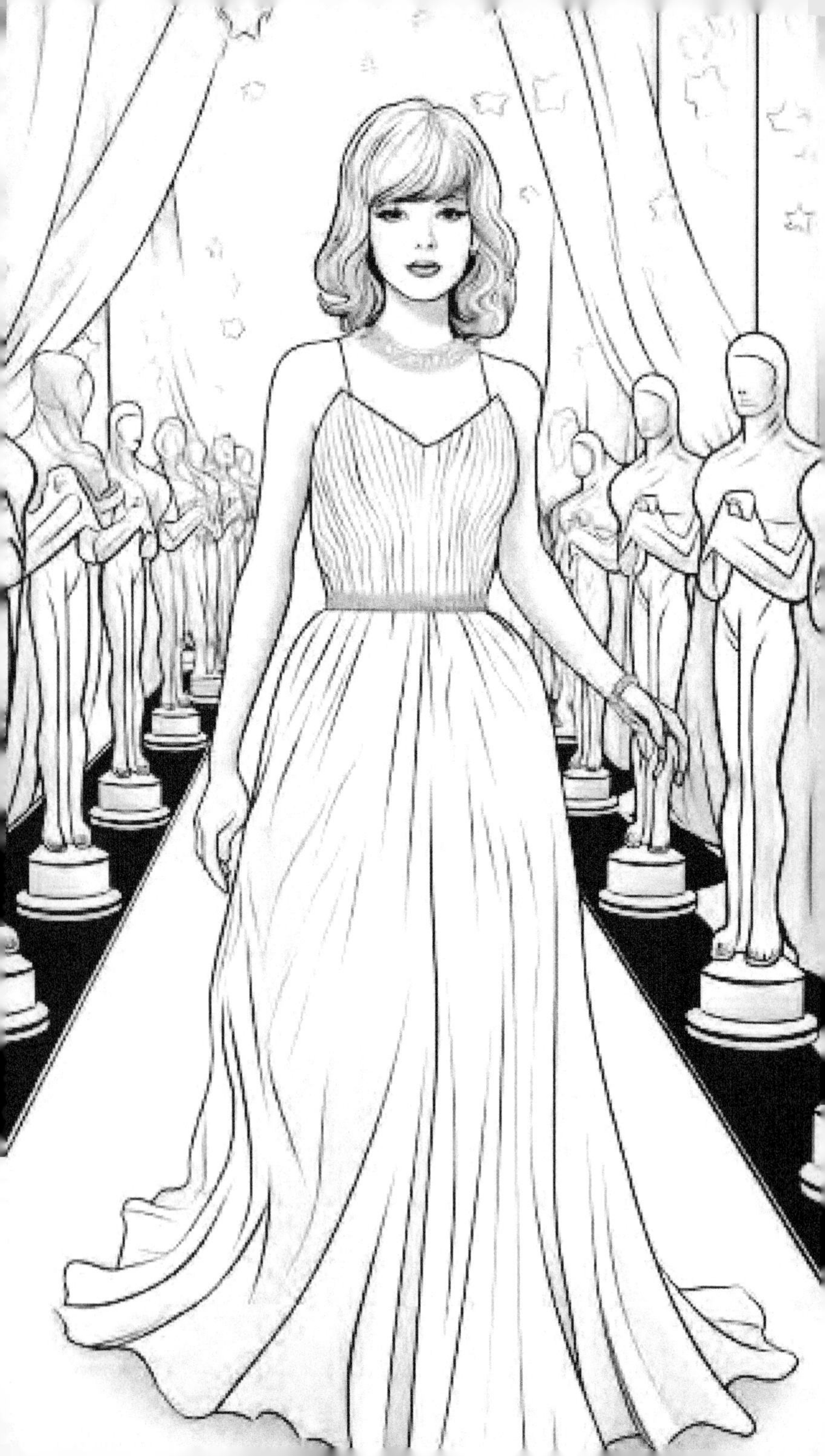

Printed in Great Britain
by Amazon